Renewing the Vows

D1509144

Renewing the Vows

Poems by Peter Schmitt

David Robert Books

Published by David Robert Books
P.O.Box 541106
Cincinnati, OH 45254-1106

ISBN: 9781933456713
LCCN: 2007926103

Poetry Editor: Kevin Walzer
Business Editor: Lori Jareo

Visit us on the web at www.davidrobertbooks.com

Acknowledgements

Art & Understanding. "Asking For It"

Bellevue Literary Review. "Thanksgiving: Visiting My Brother on the Ward"

Center. "Packing Plant"

Crab Orchard Review. "The Ropes"

Dogwood. "Cat in a Hurricane," "St. Anthony and My Father's Glasses," "Swimming Naked with the Quakers"

The Drunken Boat. "Mascot"

The Hudson Review. "Carib," "Field Guide," "First Time," "Missionaries in Oman: Collecting Shells," "The Namesake," "Sleeping Through the Fire," "Trial," "Winter Memory, Miami"

The Hurricane Review. "On Switching, After 25 Years, from Hard to Soft Contact Lenses," "Prophecy"

Indiana Review. "Blisters"

The Kenyon Review. "The Bench"

The New Criterion. "Renewing the Vows"

Poetry Kanto. "Two Suitors Dueling for Emily Dickinson"

The Seattle Review. "Lovers Lane"

Shenandoah. "Confederate Soldier, Kennesaw Mountain, July 1864"

The Southern Review. "The Lighthouse and the Turtles," "Modern Transit," "One Night," "The Wallet"

Tigertail. "Exiles," "The Perfect Child"

upstreet. "Questions for Robert Hershey"

"Mascot" was originally published in the chapbook, *To Disappear* (Pudding House).

The author would like to thank The Florida Arts Council for its generous support.

Special thanks to Jeffrey Harrison, for his always attentive reading of these poems, and for helping locate the cover image.

And gratitude to my editors, Kevin Walzer and Lori Jareo, for their commitment to my work.

in memory of my father

Contents

I.

Winter Memory, Miami

The kitchen dark but for the dim fluorescent,
my father bends to the thermometer
at the window. Later, outside, the crescent
moon dangling, slowly turning he monitors
the speed of the wind, if there is any wind,
while I stand in the chill of the open door.
Over his pajamas he wears a thin
jacket, and I don't let him see me there.

Somewhere in far rows lies this year's crop, a veil
of ice descending each leaf. And sprinklers
click through the minutes like crickets, casting
their drops as if from the hand of a priest,
while still further out, the smudge pots flicker,
faceless jack o' lanterns strewn across the fields.

Packing Plant

They must have thought I was spying on them,
my father's employees in the packing plant—
me, the boss's kid, scribbling during breaks
inside the latticed cab of a forklift.
How could I tell them those notes were poetry?

I could barely convince myself. But still
I filled the pages of the little pad,
while the place roared around me: trucks backing in,
dirt from the fields still caked in their treads; washes
and steam, groan of conveyor belts; the shouts,

the clatter of cans rattling down a chute,
hiss of boilers, and all of it echoing—
but whatever I found the concentration
to write about, it was never the plant
or its people: not the ladies on the line

in their yellow rubber boots and gloves, hairnets,
pulling, like editors, each tomato
gone soft or black or too small, shifting their weight
when their hips then knees then backs began to ache;
not Willie Cunningham, who steered a forklift

with one long black finger, who could whirl it
on a Liberty dime he'd been at it
so long, while I couldn't even drive a car
yet, banging the forks against the pallets;
Willie, who in a couple of years would lose

his testicles to cancer, my father
visiting him in the hospital, as I
waited in the car. None of it seemed worth
writing about, not even my own job,

trundling the emptied produce bins to storage,

building them to the rafters forty feet high—
not that, or the way the lunchtime whistle
would carry like a train's, shaking the beams
of the little whitewashed churches down the road,
and bring the workers forward from the dark—

and maybe I really *was* spying on them,
and just didn't know it: too busy stacking
stanzas like bins all the way to the sky—
until the next truck rumbled in with its load
and I shifted, awkwardly, into gear.

Renewing the Vows

My father, who will be dead in seven months,
and my mother are renewing their vows

in the nineteenth-century New England church
they married in, thirty-eight Octobers back.

The few of our small family are there,
my brother, my father's sister, her friend,

a couple of cousins. My mother, smiling
almost shyly it seems, has yet to take

her eyes off my father, who stands there trembling
a little, partly from the tumor, partly

from emotion which the tumor's location
has only exacerbated these days.

I would like for my father to return
my mother's gaze, but he is staring off

in another direction, his shoulders
perceptibly shaking, past the minister,

past the altar, as if he doesn't have to
look at my mother to know that she is there

and will be there. Even as he speaks his part
his eyes are somewhere else, some far corner,

and he is waiting there until, at last,
her hand reaches his for the final passage

of the ceremony, before the book
closes and there are no more words to repeat.

The Lighthouse and the Turtles

The restaurant converted from an old lighthouse
was one of my parents' favorite places
and, after about the age of five, mine too.
Just inside the front door, a long, dark green tank
with bubbling filters held so many turtles
they seemed to be crawling over each other,
in some drowsy, dreamlike attempt to climb out.
If I stood on my toes my nose could touch
the cool glass. I was too young to know about
turtle *steak*, or turtle *soup*. And late one night
when the restaurant burned to the ground, the word
arson meant nothing, and I didn't ask
if any people were hurt or killed, or if
it would reopen. All I could think of
were the turtles—and I pictured the fire
melting the tank, and the creatures riding
a great spilling wave down onto the floor,
through the legs of the tables, out the door
all the way down the sand to the ocean...
And late one night years later, when my neighbor
armed himself with a rifle and three handguns
and set his apartment ablaze, as we ran
from the building the scene played out in the slow
motion of something you cannot believe
is happening. We watched then from the pool
as that corner of the top floor burned, the way
the flames must have raced up the wooden stairs
of the lighthouse, and the abandoned beacon
flared, one last time. Like ships at sea, we waited,
staring at a code we'd never read before.

Trial

in memory of my father

You are in for another
of what is now twenty-six

MRI's, and while we wait
we think of you in the tube,

already a technician
favorite: they know the music

you like—classical—eager
to try a new tape for you

and we know, though we do not
say so, how each of these scans

amounts to a trial run,
a preparation, hard now

to imagine, as you come
wobbling out, coltish, gaining

your legs, smiling your faithful,
brave smile, how this visit makes

yet one more dress rehearsal
for the ultimate tunnel,

up that slow conveyor belt
where the only sounds will be

not voices or instruments
but the crematory's flames,

busy, thorough, trying to
take their full measure of you.

First Time

She came as a wrestler, lithe in kneepads
and helmet, to the Halloween party
I hadn't even planned on attending

and so came as myself, whatever that was
at 24. And I was about to leave
when she stopped me at the edge of the dance floor.

It was only in my bed some hours later
when I asked if I could see her again
that she told me she was married, and I thought,

So this is how it feels. And how it felt
was simply strange, as I listened to her talk
about her husband, about the cases

that took him to Mexico, and the affairs
she had known about throughout their nine years
together. How tonight was the first time,

she claimed, climbing back into the tanktop,
that she had ever tried it for herself.
And I suppose I had nothing to lose

or gain by believing her, as I did.
We met again for lunch a few days later,
but I knew it was only politeness,

a formality, as we lingered, smiling
shyly across a pitcher of sangria,
half-finished. Something had been decided

that had nothing to do with me, whoever
I might have been... I would see her one last time,
while out running on a warm December day.

I realized I'd turned down her block, then saw her
leaning back on the concrete steps, between
her husband's legs, her arms propped on his knees,

his draped over her shoulders in the way
a sweater might be loosely tied. She seemed
to be laughing at something he just said,

almost as if she had fallen backwards,
and he had been there all ready to catch her.

Carib

I think of the girl from Port Antonio...
Blue Mountains, they called them. But they were always
so shrouded in cloud I could never tell why.
And I remember that old colonial
house, the meals we fixed on the seamed butcher block—
how her skin came to taste of the spices
we used: the nutmeg, and scotch bonnet chilies,
the cinnamon, ginger, and thyme, and the pork
glazed in their marinade. *Tabula rasa*
you could call our life then, though we wouldn't
have thought so. We kept bringing dishes, loading
our arms: the black beans, the calabaza.
The house still stands. Clouds, sometimes, drift right on
    through.
But now I know why they call those Mountains Blue.

The Bench

It's all like a bad riddle, our widow friend
said at the time. *If a tree falls in the woods
and kills your husband, what can you build from it?*
That she was speaking quite literally
we did not know until the day months later
the bench arrived, filling that foyer space
in the house the neighbors pitched in to finish.

She'd done it, she said, for the sake of the boys,
and was never more sure of her purpose
than when they were off, playing in the woods
their father loved, somewhere out of earshot
and she would be struggling in with groceries.
For her, it was mostly a place to rest
such a weight, where other arms might have reached

to lift what they could. Or like the time we knocked
at her door, and finding it just ajar,
cautiously entered the sunstruck hallway,
and saw her sitting there staring into space,
before she heard our steps and caught herself,
turning smiling toward us, a book left
lying open on the bench beside her.

The Wallet

I might have seen it first, the wallet just off
the curb on the main drag of Old Orchard Beach,

but my friend and I split the cash—two hundred
and eight dollars, I will always remember—

down the middle, without considerable
soul-searching. Instead we searched the wallet,

its hidden compartments, for even more,
not so sold on our luck not to push it.

Since before dawn we'd thumbed across the state
on our day off, hours that now seemed meaningful

and all the hours before them, the bedwetters,
momma's boys, little tyrants we'd left behind,

the few pathetic hundreds of dollars
we would make for the summer, not wanting

to calculate the rate per hour. And we would
do nothing so crass as to spend our windfall,

all afternoon and night in that resort town,
an untouchable gift or compensation

for our conditions, a bonus perhaps.
Or to spend any words on it, already

become the unspoken subject between us
as we walked the miles and miles in darkness

on the two-lane, hearing noises in the woods,
to make it back by sunup. Where later,

into a brown padded mailer, we would place,
carefully, everything else: the credit cards

already cancelled; license; family
snapshots; the love letter, from his wife

probably; the errant wallet itself.
And then, with magic marker, to write the name,

which I forgot the instant the package
slipped from my hand and tumbled down the chute.

We knew, but never said to one another,
how in a few days, the ruined vacation

behind him, his heart would bounce a moment.
Then he would check, impulsively, the lining

of the wallet, on the longshot chance that we,
just maybe, might surprise him, that we wouldn't

turn out to be exactly who we were.

On Switching, After 25 Years, from Hard to Soft Contact Lenses

Tempting, to view this trade—those brittle shells,
like the fixed, tinted glass of your childhood bear,
for these grapeskins of rubbery jelly—
as a wakening, to see the world itself
anew, less rigidly, yield your dry-eyed stare
to a slippery, aqueous membrane
where all is surprise. But all that's changed,
of course, is the chemistry of your eye.
You're older. And all your small conceit reveals
is a wish, in fact, for the world to gaze on you
through a lens more pliable, forbearing,
forgiving, in the face of your decline.
Your doctor tells you to blink more, keep the tears
coming. It shouldn't be hard to comply.

II.

Prophecy

(Hurricane Cleo, 1964)

Whatever the storm can hurl at the family,
this, someday, you will write about: how X marks the spot
in tape on the windows, sandbags hide the Welcome mats,
and four and their dog huddle in the darkened hall on pillows
and blankets, the transistor radio screeling in and out,
the house breathing through one just-open jalousie,
while overhead, the little weathervane horse goes round and
    round
its tight corral, like a key some giant hand keeps turning.

And then, how the father leads his children out into the night,
the palms twitching, to see that everything is still all right,
before the winds start coming round again. And again inside,
to ride out sleepless the rest of the way till morning—
when the light reveals the severed branches and downed
    power lines,
but all about and in the house intact—except the small black
Pegasus, vanished on the air, which the boy will set out after,
and not know well enough to come inside from chasing.

The Namesake

It wasn't until my twenties finally
that I met him, my namesake—or middle name
at any rate—one evening when my parents
invited him for dinner. Retired
recently, never married, he lived alone
across town in, according to my father
a nice, spacious apartment. And while he seemed
a lonely man, he had seen the world, or
much of it, and possessed an elegance
one might emulate were it not the product
of natural gifts and long experience.
Through drinks and then dinner he and my father
talked about the war, my mother and I
listening with interest. There was much laughter
and stories we had never heard before,
a warm, glowing bubble settling over us.
But not once were words spoken about the crash.
He, of course, would have been the one to breach
the matter, if just in passing: the forced
landing, and then my father somehow freeing
himself from the wreckage. Only to see
his copilot, this man sitting next to me,
still pinned inside the cockpit. The smell of fuel.
And then my father smashing the glass, with what
he doesn't remember—his hand?—and pulling
his friend across the tarmac wavy with heat,
thirty seconds later the tanks igniting…
Before he left, he raised a toast, this man
I would never see again. And at the door
they hugged, a little awkwardly, one last time,
nodding as if to say, yes: this is how
the world left us, one who gave, and one who never
could begin to repay. And then he was gone,

my namesake, leaving me to learn, on my own,
just how one carries that kind of debt, with grace.

One Night

Twenty years, is it, since that summer day
we hitchhiked across the state, stuffed our packs
in a bus depot locker, then stumbled
stoned out of the concert only to find
the depot itself locked tight for the night—

And tired, confused, lost in a city
we did not know, it was jail, a park bench
or the Y if we wanted to sleep, back
to the highway before sunup. The night clerk
glanced blankly at our few dollars, all we had,

almost, then led us up some creaking stairs
to a large common room, with beds in rows
on facing walls. Men slept, some snored in all
but two, rather three, as an old man sat slumped
in the one next to ours, his feet on the floor,

head down, and mumbling. He looked up at us
as we pulled off our shoes and shook our blankets,
the fumes of some bottle still over him.
But before we had even settled on
the sheets, he began to speak, softly, slowly,

You're good boys, you're good boys, over and over,
in a kind of chant, just loud enough for us
to hear, not to wake any of the others,
stopping only briefly when we asked him
to let us sleep. Then, as if forgetting,

he'd start again, the same phrase repeated,
incantatory, just as we were drifting
off. Until finally, shaking our heads, we
rose from our beds and in the open window

leaned looking down at the empty street, the drone

continuing behind us, the figure
still hunched, feet flat, not once allowing himself
the privilege of lying down. Before dawn,
when a bus at last swung into view, we left
that room, the words still coming from the bed,

You're good boys, more plea than statement of fact,
and we left that city that locks its depot
fast at night, not wanting to think about
what other doors he might have been locked out of,
what other boys he had met that made him

want to believe so certainly in us.

Asking For It

It was already late when he wandered in.
He could have chosen the gurney-wide front door
in that dorm that had been an infirmary,
an electric and I-V socket open-

mouthed, halfway up the wall. He came, instead,
without knocking, through the adjoining bathroom
from the small party next door. I was still
at my desk despite the music and voices,

and though he looked familiar I did not know
his name till he slipped into the recliner
and started to talk. I put my pen down.
It *was* late, after all; I could pick it up

tomorrow. His need for conversation—
with a stranger, even—seemed more pressing
than whatever filled the paper at my hand.
I don't remember what we talked about—

his friend, my neighbor, no doubt, but a couple
hours passed, while I wondered when he might
be returning next door, the stereo
now lower, the voices fewer. But on

he stayed, merely smiling when I yawned and looked
at the bed. He asked if couldn't he just sleep
right there, in the chair. Though puzzled by now,
I assured him that the tattered La Z Boy

was famous for early morning rescues:
friends too frathouse drunk to find their own beds,
or my own resort to chivalry when dates
had missed their rides. So, with borrowed blanket,

radiator banging at winter's chill,
he stretched out, twisting and turning a bit
as I quickly undressed, stopping this time
at t-shirt and underwear, before hurtling

beneath the electric blanket with a book.
The other blanket kept moving. At last
he said he thought he'd try the floor, the throw rug
in some abstract Aztec pattern on the cold,

black hospital tile. For maybe a chapter
or more he lasted there, still shifting, squirming,
but the real story never occurred to me
until he asked, conceding that chilled air sinks,

if I would terribly mind his sharing
my single bed—small-framed, he pointed out
what little room he'd take—and then exactly
what I said I don't recall, something about

how restless I could be, how I wouldn't want
to disturb *his* sleep... But the message must have
finally sunk in, for with no further word
he climbed back in the chair and nodded off.

Thus ended an exchange that surely ranks
among the most polite in all the annals
of come-ons and rejections. Yet of my friends,
who among us, more times than he might admit,

had not tried every rhetorical means
for one night of speechless gratification—
but with a *woman*. That this unlikely source
lay dreaming, as it were, of my underclothes

as a white cotton flag to be hoisted
above the fortress, did I see something

of myself in his method? By morning
he had vanished, the blanket neatly folded,

and I never heard his name again until,
a few years after, late one night on the phone
with my old neighbor, with whom I'd kept up:
he mentioned that his friend (did I remember?)

had caught the virus and would soon be gone…
Could he have been infected even then,
I wondered, and heard confirmed what I had
only imagined: that basic scene replayed,

and not always with identical results,
a hundred, five hundred times, in different
bedrooms, other parties. Here, near the end,
my friend was saying, as the brain itself

fell open to attack, the fat cells there
were busy dumping stored-up LSD
and these last days passed in a bath of acid
flashbacks. What could one wish him but a good trip…

But now, from this distance that we call safe,
if in some eyes he was asking for it,
the one promise in promiscuity,
how can I not feel, were he asking for

anything, staring up at me so early
one morning from an icy infirmary
floor, that it was, finally, for nothing
that I—nothing anybody—could give him.

Mascot

for a friend with bulimia

One year in high school
as team mascot
you wore another skin,
leaping as a panther
at pep rallies
and football games,
losing your body
wholly inside another
a few hours every week,
and no one knew it was you.
The panther
had swallowed you up,
it was his problem now, his
the calories and pounds
to lose, his
the image in the tubas
and cymbals, he was the one
to make others laugh
and cheer.
At the end of the night
when he vomited you
back up, the panther
could hide
in your closet,
nothing but skin,
without spirit,
staring out at you
with his comforting,
vacant eyes.

St. Anthony and My Father's Glasses

My mother isn't Catholic, but ever since
my father's stay at Mercy Hospital
she prays to St. Anthony, to help locate
what otherwise refuses to be found.

He was just out of lung surgery, and back
in his room, but his glasses were nowhere.
Not with his clothes, not in my mother's purse.
It hurt to breathe from where they had spread his ribs,

and all he could do was watch TV—but not
without the glasses. It was just about then
that Sister Nancy from Patient Services
sailed breezily in, habit cutting a wake

like a catamaran, and knew right away
what to do, complete with a rhyme to invoke
the busy saint. And sure enough, within
mere minutes, the little verse much repeated,

the missing spectacles revealed themselves,
peering from beneath a blanket on a shelf.
In the years following, St. Anthony
has proven himself reliable and prompt:

keys, address book, a cameo (received
one anniversary), airline tickets
the morning of a flight. My mother's careful
not to solicit saintly intervention

except in matters of clear importance,
and he has never failed her, she reports.
Even Anthony, of course, can't stop the loss
of certain things once and for all—for instance,

my father (the tumor hidden in his brain
soon unmistakably there), but prayer, it seems,
is like valor: discretion's the better part—
you ask for what you reasonably can have,

and somehow learn to live without the rest.

Sleeping Through the Fire

When the flames lit up the woods across the lane
I failed to move, lost in some adolescent
slumber. Soon the tallest pines were involved,

but there in that second story bedroom
not once did I waken to the neighbors' shouts—
not as the wind shifted toward the house,

and they ran with CO_2 and buckets
spilling from the lake. Though the walls were thin
I never felt my family downstairs,

their bolting from rooms and slamming of doors.
And through an open window, somehow I missed
the volunteers' truck taking the corner,

the squeal of its brakes and dispersal of men.
Instead, I floated like smoke above the scene,
there at sixteen, even with the fire rising

to the next level. And no one looked for me.
In the morning, I would see the black ring—
the damp needlebed, and charred limbs—but that night

they left me in my room, where I might sleep
a little longer, before unexcusing
daylight called me down at last into the world.

Lovers Lane

Ours was a "love-car" out of Lowell's "Skunk Hour,"
and we could fog the glass with the best of them,
those kids half our age, and half our resting time,
between acts. Was there anything unobscured,
from ourselves if not from the world, car shaking
from side to side as if in denial,
the dashboard dials like our future dimming, while
LOVE 94 took requests, some heartbreaking.
From this distance even your cry of alarm
seems somehow off-key, that night sticky-warm
with most of our clothing down past our knees,
their smirking surprise, badges, lights in our eyes
and shouting, needlessly, for us to move on,
the steam at our windows already half-gone.

Field Guide

*"…and whatever the man called every living creature,
that was its name."*

Because it wasn't enough
just to see him—
we had to know his name—
on the screened-in porch
we glanced back and forth
from Peterson's *Field Guide*
to a dead treetop
by the shore
where a bird whose size
we'd seen nowhere near
the lake in years
perched motionless staring
at the blurry text
of the not-yet-frozen water.
And naturally
the very moment we settled
on the color plate, finally,
making positive I.D.,
was exactly when we missed
the dive he was made for—
for as our gaze
lifted off the page
he was already rising up
and beating away
with dinner flapping
in his talons,
leaving us his name
in a wake of spray—osprey!—
"whose dive,"
Peterson's advises,
"is steep, *feet*-first,
spectacular."

Confederate Soldier, Kennesaw Mountain, July 1864

In my field glasses the little steeple
of our church just pokes above the treeline;
and I remember how the whole town gathered
the day we brought the bell down for the melting.
And the foundrymen swore they heard a tolling
when the great fires did their work. Now each morning
I stroke the barrel of my Spiller and Burr
for luck, because I know God clothes himself
in shades of gray; and if my aim is sure
I also know that somewhere north of here
church bells will sound out once again, and a town
will congregate, in dark suits, buttons shining.

III.

The Perfect Child

You wore it so lightly, the plastic halo
that kept, at bathtime, the burning shampoo
from your eyes. But then, for your blessed parents,
diligent, vigilant, you were their angel.
The suds came down around you like a curtain.

By the time it fit too tightly round your head
you were more than ready to fling it off,
to stand now in the shower like a man
and manage your own ablutions—even if
it did mean eyes, nose, everything on fire.

Questions for Robert Hershey

(1954-1970)

Aren't you still sleeping in the back of class,
not beneath some towering oak and the grass
of a Carolina graveyard? And do you
still answer your colonel father with "Sir,"
and have you let your crewcut grow out? And weren't
those your hands working the wires beneath the dash
of the Mustang? And how did I know, when word
raced the halls, that they weren't on the wheel, those hands,

but a girl in the crowded back seat? And she
held tight to you, didn't she, when the needle
passed one-ten, and the Mississippi freeway
fell away, and for just a moment—somewhere
midair?—she could see in your eyes no regret,
and wasn't it the last thing she'd ever see?

Thanksgiving: Visiting My Brother on the Ward

Behind the thick, crosshatched glass of the cruiser,
my brother, back for the holiday, breathes
more slowly. A phalanx of uniforms
cloaks the open door, murmuring to him
where he sits. The carving knife is somewhere
out of reach, none of us so much as scratched.
Inside, the bound bird cools on the butcher block.

Later that night I move through many doors, each
locking behind me, each inlaid with the same
heavy glass as the squad car. Through the last
I see my brother's face, fixed as on a graph,
ordinate, abscissa. When he sees mine
he retreats from the common room to his own,
a bare cell he shares with a narrow bed.

He will not speak to me, at first. His fingers
move in perpetual chafe, like a mantis,
his lifelong nervous habit, the edges
of a newspaper shredded on the bed.
This time, his eyes say, we have betrayed him
as never before. This time, he seems to say,
he cannot find a way to forgive us.

At last I persuade him to join the others
finishing the meal, their plastic utensils
working the meat, their low voices broken
by stray whoops of inappropriate laughter.
We sit, though, in a separating silence,
my brother's hand already eroding
his napkin, eyes distant with medication.

If only he were faithful to himself
and took his daily pills… But what is the point

of such a constancy when the world itself
has so profoundly turned away? As tonight
I will leave him here, leave all of them here,
the psychotics and depressives, my brother,
to lie on their beds and stare at their ceilings,

and I know that for at least this visit
he will not come home, where our parents now sit
in darkness, their faces streaked and damp. And when
we drive him to the airport, an unmarked
police car following as an escort,
he might be a foreign dignitary
bearing developments back to his country…

For now, though, it is just two brothers, beneath
a glaring bulb. The expression on his face
would ask, *Have you gotten what you came for?*
And again I have no answer for him.
But there, at the floor of the bed, all around
the room, are crumbs of paper, as if he were
leaving a trail by which he might be found.

Camp Stories

1. The Ropes

The night they tied my brother to a tree,
someone ran to call me from my cabin.
But I got there—as usual—too late;
they'd let him go, and he'd run off to hide,
and cry, not to return until morning.

But I found the tree, around which the kids
in his bunk had danced, and laughed, calling him names
like *Retard! Dummy!* and I found the ropes,
coiled at the base of the tree like snakes.
That summer, we'd learned about tying knots,

and how a tourniquet stops the flow of blood—
except for my brother, who couldn't, was slow,
who to this day can't tie a knot or make
a bow, yet may know as much about them
as any there that night, or anyone not.

2. Blisters

"And last but not least—Mr. Impetigo-
Man!" That's how Newt Jackson introduced me
at our social with the girls' cabin—Newt,
our cocky, cutup black impresario,
who laughed as my face reddened past its blotches.

The skin had blistered from that night in a tent
I'd rigged badly on the side of a mountain.
An unexpected downpour sent running mud
through the flaps as I tried to pillow the head
of my brother with my own, and couldn't.

But Newt was mostly trying to impress
a girl, in fact the corresponding leader
of their bunk, a beautiful fourteen-year-old,
tall, with a perfect and imposing Afro,
like a huge brown sun risen above the lake.

Her name was Attalah, and Newt would draw out
the syllables in a reverential hush,
stressing their delicacy, and she seemed
to possess an elegance and stature
beyond her years. And there I was, skinny,

small, not yet pubescent, braces on my teeth,
thick glasses, bandages—a white boy contagious
with impetigo. The other girls tried
not to laugh. And was it the Quaker camp,
the Vermont mountains, 1973,

that allowed a lovely black girl to reach out
to an embarrassed white boy, to take my hand,
and say, "We're pleased to meet you. Come over
sometime, and let us get to know you better"—?
I never did, of course. Or get to know her—

until, maybe, ten years later, on a plane
skimming through *People* magazine, something
about a dance troupe, and Dr. King's daughter,
and there, suddenly, the name, the syllables—
Attalah—that face, and then the story—

how she was all of six, her mother, sisters
sitting with her, the Audubon Ballroom,
all eyes on her father, no one's on the man
with the shotgun—how she saw everything
that followed. And there I was, back at the lake,

and fourteen, knowing only what Newt knew—
that she was impossibly beautiful,
and knew more than we did—and how easily
she laughed, at some silly thing Newt just said,
and I was laughing too, first time all day.

3. Swimming Naked with the Quakers

When everyone started shedding their clothes
at the coed swim, it should have been any
adolescent's fantasy: the counselors

from the girls' camp across the lake, nineteen,
twenty years old (same age as my students now),
the same ones we would hear at night in the woods

with *our* counselors (whose showered bodies we saw
every day). And even more compelling,
the few bold girls from our sister cabin,

our age, who dared to drop their bikini tops
and bottoms, whom my bunkmate Newt had observed
sunning themselves invitingly on their dock.

It should have been a scene I plunged into,
like something out of Bosch, but I was fourteen,
puberty had not yet had its way with me,

I had yet to sow my Quaker oats, and
the small percussion bombs of impetigo
still ravaged my face. It wasn't meant to be

exciting, really, at all: just the Quaker
bent for the natural, the unadorned—
all summer I'd opted for the *clothing* side

of *clothing-optional* at our waterfront,
where the only females were a few nurses
old enough to be my grandmother. No,

for the two, three hundred men and women
undressing before my eyes and splashing
into the dappled lake, there was nothing

remarkable about it; but I was
simply not that enlightened, and certainly
not that unimpressed—so I retreated,

to the rec room above the beach, where ping-pong
beckoned, and a few other reticent kids,
and taking then the side of a table

that afforded me a commanding view
of the whole lakefront—I may have been shy
but I was no fool—took up a paddle,

which in less pacifist camps might have doubled
as an instrument of discipline, but here,
as I swung it past my face, seemed like a fan,

with the sudden heat rising from below.

4. Bedwetter

When the uric acid seemed to drift like steam
off Andrew's mattress, the other kids complained.

By then the smell had settled in the very
timbers of the cabin, in the pine beams,

and deeper, into our pillows, our soap.
That's when we pulled the mattress from the bunk

and dragged it into the sun, the yellow stain
like a reflection, the sun in miniature.

Andrew was smaller than his peers, a crier,
and he cried now, his shame publicly exposed.

He was also the cook's grandson, and sometimes
disappeared—for ice cream, we suspected.

That night, after dinner but before dark,
before we brought the mattress in from drying,

Andrew's grandpa appeared out of nowhere—
a white-haired, feisty bantam of a man—

and drunk, and came at me with a roundhouse right
that would have landed had Vinnie not stepped in—

my junior counselor, sixteen—and caught his arm.
Later we learned that Andrew was actually

seven years old, not nine like his bunkmates,
and something in the place began to smell

worse than piss, and for the rest of that summer
I double-checked the bad camp food three times

a day, and never walked alone at night.
A quarter century later and I hope

that Andrew has survived despite his family;
the old guy's likely dead; though I hated him

then, I understand now he was only
defending his family honor, and name—

what else could he do—now that both were soiled,
not by Andrew, but some smartass college punk

who barely knew what it took to feed himself,
much less a camp—men and boys, hundreds of them.

My Father's Obituary

In the first panic
of seizure and paramedics,
of the bathroom fall
and race to the hospital,
I doubted my composure—
my ability to compose—
when the time actually came.
So in the relative calm
of his return home
I wrote about him,
then buried the draft
in a bottom drawer. After
a month passed, another,
and still my father
hung on, through emergencies
and reprieves, surgeries
and radiation, my tribute
came to seem a rebuke—
not of him but of me,
a kind of mockery
that I'd doubted the life
within him. He'd have laughed,
probably, if he knew.
But I knew.
And when a year had gone
and he endured, the long
page each day went off
like the cheap watch I'd tossed
in the desk with it,
whose alarm I'd somehow set
but couldn't undo...
And then one day
it was ready, needing
just some minor editing,

those last months
a discreet mention
in a few words—added
at the head
of the notice—as if the man
only with his death began,
or, for me, began over,
now that every
easy summary
was entirely behind me.

Exiles

From the kitchen, she hears her Cuban neighbors
gathered for *Navidad*, cousins, grandkids,
abuelas, such sweet commotion—the pig, glazed
as a suckling skewered on its spit, children
smacking the pregnant piñata, the old folks
recalling the lights along the Malecon—
as she carries plates to the table, her son,
still unmarried, sprawls, dozing at halftime.

She has her own Havana memories.
That first trip, her son barely six months old;
neither she nor his father saying much
on the short flight, just watching the mountains
as the island neared. Then the second, too soon
after the brother came along, who lives
too far now to make it in. She remembers
the clinic's water-stained ceiling, then the room
beginning to submerge, her husband's face
rising out of focus, voices receding.

Her son should be married by now. There should be
children, filling her apartment with sound,
clamor, leaving her things to turn over,
smiling or frowning, after they all troop home.
Instead, he will kiss her goodnight, close the door
gently behind him, where she sits among
empty place settings, little dog at her feet,
making faintly restive queries in its sleep.

Cat in a Hurricane

(Andrew, Category 5)

Those hours I hunkered with radio
and flashlight in the bedroom closet, waiting
for the thrashing palm to shatter the window,
two-year-old Chelsey spent blissfully swatting
a toy back and forth, now and then peering
in where I sat, strangely. Only at first light
of dawn, the winds fallen to eighty or so,
did she stare wide-eyed at the ravages
taken with the world she knew, trees still savagely
flayed and shaken. That was a dozen years ago.
Today with the thunder's first throat-clearing
it's under the bed, alert to every sound
and tremor in the house. *Oh sweetheart, you're right:*
there's so much more to be afraid of now.

Modern Transit

1. Rollerblade

Those who glide across the campus,
darting, following each other
with the sure synchronicity
of fish in a school—lurch into
the classroom now, bumping past chairs
and fumbling out of their backpacks
as if wrestling off parachutes.
Suddenly a whole head taller,
it's clear they don't belong here, wheels
literally spinning, their blades
aimed at the lectern and Walkmen
garlanding their necks, and you share
their relief when the hour is up,
each a tanned and toned Mercury
no longer detained, bearing off
you can only guess what message.

2. Bungee

To drop,
dizzyingly,
from a webwork
of bridge, the line
paying out as
if from inside
you, then, both taut
and elastic,
catching you up,
setting you down
in a series
of descending
bounces, till you
come to a rest
and, looking up,
can see the line
as something made
of your life—well,
what have you done
that every
day a spider
doesn't?—Only
the spider knows
how the line holds
him fast.

3. Personal Submersible Vehicle

Only seven thousand dollars
in the new Neiman's catalogue,
its hatch fits over your torso
leaving your legs exposed, like some
vision of the future that Verne
might have dreamed: half man, half machine.
Neiman's recommends his 'n' her
models, but solo is the way
to really go—down, down, your eyes
fish-placid behind the thick glass,
no concern about the pressure,
no interfering bubbles, no
need to communicate with boat
or partner, just drifting, down to
previously unimagined
depths of self-immersion, lovely.

4. With Motion Sensors

Now that lights blink on with each stride
deeper into the stacks (thanks to
the library's cost-slashing plan),
it's hard not to feel a little
like a god, your each step a kind
of *Fiat Lux*, all of knowledge
opening before you. Of course
the whole of it nearly as fast
goes to black in your wake, as if
the world indeed (or this small part
of it) depended upon you,
so the idea is to keep
moving forward. Or, barring that,
just moving, a limb preferably,
as to pause here with merely eyes
moving no longer seems enough.

Two Suitors Dueling for Emily Dickinson

(after an idea suggested by one of my students, misreading a poem)

It will end disappointingly
for either of them, naturally.

Even now as they count off steps
like pentameter, their backs stiff

to one another like bookends,
they're wondering why they are here,

just what it is they think they see
in the odd girl, her stare intense

and inward. Each would like to turn
in his tracks right now, and say *Hey!*

What are we doing? Are we nuts?
Can I buy you a drink instead?—

but it's the nineteenth century,
and don't they know it. She, of course,

has retreated to her bedroom
upstairs, where she sits rapt in thought

at her quaint writing desk, and not
until this moment realizing

she's left the window wide open.

Missionaries in Oman: Collecting Shells

We slept on the roof, under towels dipped
every two or three hours in water
from the cistern. The children never uttered
a word. Nights were a kind of reprieve; it dropped
to one hundred and ten. But on weekends
we roamed our cloudless desert beach, looking
for shells, and the sea rose above us, immense,
itself like the curve of an enormous whelk,
cerulean. The ones we couldn't find
in the book we shipped in a box to England.
When they came back, they were ours to christen.
The first, my husband named for me, the children
next; by now, we're almost out of family!
And we can call ourselves home, finally.

About the Author

Peter Schmitt is the author of two collections of poems, *Country Airport* and *Hazard Duty* (Copper Beech), and a chapbook, *To Disappear*, published by Pudding House in 2006. A graduate of Amherst and The Iowa Writers Workshop, he has received The Peter I.B. Lavan Younger Poets Award from The Academy of American Poets; The "Discovery"/*The Nation* Prize; and grants from The Florida Arts Council (twice), and The Ingram Merrill Foundation. His poems have appeared in *The Hudson Review*, *The Nation*, *The Paris Review*, *Poetry*, and *The Southern Review*, and are widely anthologized. His work has also been featured on National Public Radio's Writers Almanac. A contributor of poetry reviews to *The Miami Herald* and *South Florida Sun-Sentinel*, he has taught creative writing and literature at The University of Miami since 1986.

About the Artist and Cover

Everett Warner (1877-1963) was born in Iowa and after studying at The Art Students League in New York, affiliated in 1909 with The Old Lyme (Connecticut) Art Colony. A center of American Impressionism, the Art Colony flourished under the sponsorship of patron Florence Griswold, whose home is now a museum housing many of the Colony's artworks. *The Village Church* (1910, oil on canvas, 32 x 26) depicts The First Congregational Church of Old Lyme, a favorite subject of the Lyme Art Colony, and the setting for this book's title poem. When the church burned down in 1907, possibly by arson, artist Childe Hassam, also of the Lyme group, declared that only the Devil himself could be responsible for destroying such an architectural treasure. Using paintings and photographs as guides, the church was rebuilt in 1910. Warner went on to a distinguished career in painting and printmaking, and contributed significantly to the design of ship camouflage for the United States Navy in World Wars I and II.

CPSIA information can be obtained
at www.ICGtesting.com
Printed in the USA
LVOW12s0506040516

486595LV00001B/7/P